S. B Stonerook

Off the Beaten Track

Through the Big Bald, Big Horn, Shoshone, and the Rocky Mountains to

Yellowstone National Park: an accurate and concise description of the

entire trip from Ottumwa, Iowa, to Yellowstone National Park and return

S. B Stonerook

Off the Beaten Track
Through the Big Bald, Big Horn, Shoshone, and the Rocky Mountains to Yellowstone National Park: an accurate and concise description of the entire trip from Ottumwa, Iowa, to Yellowstone National Park and return

ISBN/EAN: 9783337148836

Printed in Europe, USA, Canada, Australia, Japan

Cover: Foto ©Andreas Hilbeck / pixelio.de

More available books at **www.hansebooks.com**

Off the Beaten Track.

Through the Big Bald, Big Horn, Shoshone,
and the Rocky Mountains,

TO

Yellowstone National Park.

_____

An accurate and concise description of the entire trip
from Ottumwa, Iowa, to Yellowstone
National Park and Return.

_____

BY

PROF. S. B. STONEROOK, JR., B. D.

TIPTON, IOWA.

One of the Party.

THIS BOOK I write as one of the company. What I saw each one saw. What I experienced we all experienced. At noon I wrote what happened in forenoon. In the evening, what happened in the afternoon. In the morning—the night.]

BLOOMFIELD CONTINGENT.

J. W. Stark,
Mrs. J. W. Stark,
W. J. Law.
Miss May Allender.

RED OAK CONTINGENT.

Will Thomas.
J. A. Hysham.
J. R. Anderson.
I. S. Iddings.
S. G. Hersman.

NEWMAN GROVE, NEB.
CONTINGENT.
Thos. Ostergard.
Mrs. Thos. Ostergard.
E. O. Spielberg.

GLENWOOD, IOWA.
J. F. Record.

TIPTON, IOWA.
S. B. Stonerook, Jr.

STANTON, IOWA.
J. W. Finley.
Mrs. J. Finley.

To and Fro the Wonderland of the Ages.

*   *   *   *   *

TUESDAY.

On Tuesday morning July 7th, in company with
W. J. Law, Mr. and Mrs. J. W. Stark and Miss May
Allender, of Bloomfield, Iowa, I boarded train number
three of the Chicago, Burlington and Quincy Railroad,
at Ottumwa, Iowa, for a famous journey to the wonder-
land of the ages, the celebrated Yellowstone National
Park. The day was perfect. The sun was filling
eastern Iowa with his magnificent rays, making our
hearts rejoice and each one feel at his best. After an
introduction to W. S. Parker, the genial ticket agent at
Ottumwa, and a few friendly greetings, our palace on
wheels moved on. We took luncheon at Creston, Iowa,
on chicken, cake and wine. O. J. Gibson, our obliging
manager, and P. S. Eustis, the general passenger agent
of the Burlington, were brought into the good graces
of our party at Red Oak, Iowa. They stamped and
made good our tickets for the great journey. Our
Yellowstone party was here augmented by the addition
of J. A. Hysham, J. R. Anderson, J. W. Finley and wife,
A. S. Iddings, Will. Thomas and S. G. Hersman. The
ride through Iowa was delightful. All along the road

the earth was groaning with the abundance of vegetation. At 2:20 we crossed the muddy waters of the
Missouri and passed rapidly on towards Omaha. We
reached Lincoln, Nebraska, at 5:55 after an excellent
days ride. Our party was joined at this place by
Thos. Ostergard and wife, and E. O. Spielberg of
Newman Grove, Nebraska, and J. F. Record of Glenwood, Iowa, who had accompanied his daughter to
Lincoln, and there joined our party and became our
kind and whole hearted manager after the departure
of O. J. Gibson at Sheridan, Wyoming. Here our party
was completed. We dined at the Burlington on ham,
eggs, beefsteak and chicken. After partaking of an
elegant dinner our party headed by O. J. Gibson boarded
a Pullman Sleeper, "The Clover," sent out from Chicago
on purpose by the Burlington officials for the accom-
modation of our party. 10:30 found most of our
company in their berths. The ride through north-
western Nebraska was extremely dirty. The sand
among the Sand-Hills was whirling furiously most of
the night. I thought our party would be filled up
with sand before dawn. Morning however found us
all alive.

WEDNESDAY.

The sun rose high and in its beaming way found
us spinning through a sad, sad country, acres and acres,
and thousands and thousands of acres that cannot be
irrigated stretched out in pensive quietness toward the
setting sun. Nothing can give the tourist a more vivid im-
pression of the greatness of our country, and adventurous
character of our people, as the sight of these boundless

prairies and the habitations of the hardy pioneers who are rapidly turning the buffalo sod and exposing the rich, black soil to the fertilizing action of the sun and air, and substituting for nature's scant forage abundant harvests of wheat, corn and oats. In this newer territory the towns are less frequent and smaller in size, the plains appear more nearly in their native state, only dotted here and there with the sod houses of the claim settlers. As we move on and the traveler looks out of the car window across this billowy expanse, he sees herds of cattle and sheep grazing on the rich buffalo grass and occasionally catches a glimpse of a jack rabbit trying to outspeed the iron horse. Prairie dogs in innumerable numbers sitting on their haunches like diminutive kangaroos at times entertain a whole car load of people with pleasurable excitement. The extreme north-west of Nebraska is hilly and undulating not unlike the eastern highlands.

By special request of Edgemont Company, represented by O. D. Noble, of Omaha, Nebraska, our entire party stopped off one day at Edgemont, South Dakota. We were met at depot by mayor, city officers, editors, and prominent men. After a friendly greeting we were ushered into the spacious dining parlors of the Burlington where we partook of an excellent breakfast. This city was determined to show us the wealth of their country. After a short visit in Edgemont, examining her offices and business centers, we were ushered into eight carriages and driven through a lovely portion of their agricultural community. They farm by irrigation using the water from the Cheyenne river. They showed us a marvelous growth in a country

only two years old.   High noon found us back again
in Edgemont ready for dinner at the Burlington.

At 2:30 our party left on a special day coach
to visit their famous stone quarries and grind stone
works which are located near this place.   The plant
cost $1,000,000.   They have an enormous amount of
stone.   They claim that larger quarries and stones of
finer grit are found nowhere in the world.   We saw
them turn the grind stones as the carpenter turns his
wood, and saw off slabs of stones, six slabs at a time,
as easily as one saws a board.   At the quarries they
drill by steam, and they do their heavy lifting with a steam
derrick.   They gave each of our party a little grind
stone as a souvenir.   They run our car out into one of
their finest canons where we looked down over a trestle
126 feet high.   On our homeward way we visited their
paint mills.   In the evening our party enjoyed themselves in bathing, playing pool, and taking in the sights
generally.   Our visit at Edgemont was indeed superb.
The city officials, business men, and people generally
treated us royally, they did all in their power to make
it pleasant for us   Their people are kind and generous.
All our travels around Edgemont, and entertainments
did not cost our party any money.   We were willing
to stay with them forty years if they would so contract.
The location and natural resources of Edgemont are
promising indeed.

THURSDAY.

We had breakfast at 6:10.   Gave our good people
good-bye and started for Sheridan, Wyoming.   The trip
was long, hot and tedious.   We again passed through

much poor country, we saw a herd of cattle probably 10,000 head, our engine struck a cow and helped her to turn a fine summer sault. What a pity the great North-West cannot be brought under cultivation. We arrived at Sheridan, Wyoming, at 2:05. After we had dinner at "Sheridan Inn," we took a stroll up town and got our forwarded mail and purchased postal cards and stamps for the trip. A few remained at the "Inn" to change their clothing and store away their extra baggage. O. J. Gibson our manager thus far, left our party after our first camp, on account of the serious illness of his mother. J. F. Record then assumed full charge of company. We were loathe to part with Mr. Gibson. After we had arrayed ourselves in our traveling costumes we awaited our conveyances for the great overland drive of thirty-four days. Our party thus far is standing the trip pretty well, one man sick at the "Sheridan Inn," the rest are joyous and happy. The weather here is very hot, the sun fairly boils. At five o'clock our party in five conveyances started for the famous Yellowstone National Park. The out-start was somewhat dusty. Our first camp was pitched on Soldier Creek, six miles north-west of Sheridan. Our party helped to pitch the three tents while the cooks prepared our supper of potatoes, pork, corn, cake and peaches, tea and coffee. The evening was spent in telling camp fire jokes. We had some lively music and dancing in camp. I tried my luck in firing four shots at a jack rabbit, the rabbit ran away unharmed.

FRIDAY.

We arose on July 10 at 4 o'clock, after resting six hours in a wild, wild country with not a house in sight.

After breakfast we resumed our journey at 8 o'clock. A stiff breeze fanned us nearly all day. We drove 17 miles pretty lively and put up at Dayton, Wyoming. We saw some farming country. We had dinner on the banks of Tongue River. At 2 o'clock we started for the mountains proper. We fished to-day but no fish. We walked part way up the mountains. At 5 o'clock we pitched tent, took supper and spent a pleasant eve in camp. We have a fine view over valleys below and distant plains from our camp. I took a good bath in a mountain torrent. Our party caught some fish. The nights are pleasant and cool. We saw people having short trees tied behind to their wagons to get down the mountains, the trees drag heavily on the earth and act as brakes, this is about the only way they can get down in places. We had a camp fire in the evening. We came very near having a lively fire. Rev. Stark very earnestly piled up a large pile of dead pine and set fire to it to lighten up the camp. The wind turned and blew the ascending flames towards the ladies' tent, and at times the flames rolling over the tent while the reverend gentlemen trying to protect the tent stood between the flames and the tent and shouted, fire! fire!!

SATURDAY.

Most of the party managed to get out of bed at 4:40, went down a steep canyon to a cold mountain torrent to wash their faces, then put up our beds, took down the tents and prepared for breakfast on pork, potatoes, oat meal, coffee, tea and crackers. At 6:30 camp broke and off we were for the mountains, most of the male part of our company walked up the mountain and left the ladies ride. This has been a hard forenoon. The "Big Horn" on the east are hard to ascend. I walked all forenoon. We camped at noon on the summit or very near the summit of the mountains, at a little spring. The water was fine but the flies all tried to kill us. We passed a flock of sheep, 10,000, that were on their way to the head-waters of Tongue River. We also passed a drove of horses. I met a man on the very summit of " Big Horn Mountains," who was raised in Cedar County, Iowa, only 14 miles from my home. Our camp wagon was delayed at noon and gave us a late start for afternoon travel. Ostergard and Spielberg traveled ten miles farther than our commissary wagon in the forenoon, Ostergard walked back to get dinner, Spielberg moved on and finally fell in with another crowd who cared for him, he found us late in the evening. In places it was very dusty, we get our ears and hair so full of sand that you could grow water melons. It rained about three drops to-day, our mess wagon arrived in camp at 3:20 P. M. We took dinner immediately and pulled ten miles through the "Big Horn" Mountains. We saw some magnificent scenery, castle rocks towering sky high, immense areas of evergreens, various kinds, with many beautiful flowers growing beneath. The scenery in places is grand beyond description. From summit of the mountain we saw a small town on fire, about six houses were burned. We passed quite a few teamsters who were hauling wool, also saw a party tenting who were digging a large water ditch, passed a flock of 7,000 sheep, struck camp, had supper at 10:30 P. M., to bed at 11 o'clock and nearly froze.

SUNDAY.

After breakfast we had a little visit with a man who lived close by, then broke camp and started for a forty miles drive. We passed some beautiful water-falls and landscapes. The drive was pleasant, indeed. At noon we saw some beautiful drifts of snow on the sides of Bald Mountain. We camped at "Little Bald," I carried wood and Mr. Record, our manager, cut same for dinner. Part of our party carried their beer up into the snow-drifts to cool it off. Our trip this forenoon was cool, most too cool to be extra pleasant. At noon the drivers turned their horses out of camp and left them graze around, they never attempt to run away, we have not as yet tied them.

This day we had an excellent dinner. At 1:10 P. M. we resumed our march, after a little drive we reached summit of Bald "Mountain." Oh! what a sight we had of "Big Horn Basin" and the valley below. You could see several rivers wind their torturous ways through the various valleys. The trip down the mountain was terrific, at places we went almost straight down, and so sidling that we several times nearly upset. It took three and four men in places to keep our conveyances from turning over. We passed some magnificent canyons. We passed off the road onto a ledge of enormous rocks where we had a view that cannot be imagined. The road down the sides of the mountain was fearfully rocky, and in places so narrow and steep that if one should miss the road he would roll miles and miles into the valley below. We had much trouble getting down this mountain, we all walked most of the way. Occasionally it required two and three men to hold our wagons from rolling over and down the mountain.

A view over the "Big Horn Basin" looks sad, no vegetation and very few things of interest. We passed not a living soul on the road all day long. In the evening we caught sight of a little house far down in the valley. A shame for any man who tries to raise any family in these desolate, barren and alkali hills. We reached tent about 6:10 and camped at a beautiful spring about 3000 feet above the valley. We had a good supper of mush and milk, potatoes, ham, biscuits, tea and coffee. In the evening, Sunday, Rev. Stark of Bloomfield, Iowa, a Presbyterian minister in our party, by request, preached an excellent sermon on the grandeur of God in nature. We drilled several small holes into the ground with tent pins and placed therein lighted sperm candles. The music on this occasion sounded to me as never before. Nothing but lonely cliffs for miles and miles. At 10:45 we went to bed after spending most of the day above the clouds and among the rocks. Our party is very agreeable, some are a little lazy. We had a bad storm during the night.

MONDAY.

This morning we all washed out of a little spring about ten rods from camp, then took breakfast at 6:15. The morning is bright and cool. We have an excellent cook and he cooks well for us. Some of us have a bad cold nearly all the while, the nights change too much for us. Our camp, I named Camp Nebo. When we are

ready to eat, each one goes up to the various pots
containing the things cooked, then fills his tin plate and
goes away a little distance and sits on rocks or camp-
stools and eats.

This morning as I look back over the mountains
I see the clouds settling down along the mountain side.
We dread the trip to-day, the country through which
we pass is almost a desert. We left camp at 7:15; we
went down a pretty steep descent; we had much fun
rolling stones down the hill; we passed a very beautiful
ranchman's home in a little pocket of sunshine with a
little rain. They live in a lonely place, go to town only
once in a year, then buy enough to last them for a whole
year; the wife and children look as sound as a pine
knot.

The ride this forenoon was fearfully dirty, sometimes
you could not see the driver or the side of the road.
We drove 17 miles this forenoon; at 12 o'clock we
halted for dinner at Hardy's Ranch, here we put out
some of our laundry. We met a few pleasant people at
this place, they tried to sell us some bear skins; we
watched a large mountain fire through our field glasses,
a whole ravine full of pine shrubbery was wrapped
in a terrific blaze.

We left our camp Hardy at 2:15, crossed Shell Creek
bottoms and camped on Shell Creek. Here is a small
ranch controlled by a family named Whalley, they have
a small store. We wrote letters, washed clothing
and bathed; we spent the evening in telling stories.
A man here offered us 160 acres of land and 10 horses
for $450.00, I thought it was too cheap, situated 150
miles from nearest railroad, and mostly sage brush.

It could be irrigated, but who could live in such a lonesome and God-for-saken place. We stopped early to-day on account of water; we did some fishing and caught a fine mess of mountain trout, more than we could eat. The mosquitoes were very bad, they chased me out of bed about 1 o'clock at night.

TUESDAY.

Our cook arose at 3 o'clock, at 5:45 we were on our way from the mosquitoes' land. The drive this forenoon was long and tedious, we passed through the desert part way; it will take us six days more to cross this 100 miles desert; I had to wear goggles nearly all day; we almost up-set in several places, sage-brush without end and horse high. We were lonesome to-day. I caught two horned toads which I will send East. We camped at noon at Basin City Ferry. After luncheon J. M. Tillard of Alamo, Fremont County, Wyoming, transferred our entire company across the Big Horn River for five dollars; his family are the only people in the whole country, he expects a county seat close by before the day of judgment. This is a lonely home for his two daughters, at least 150 miles from nearest town on railroad.

This makes our seventh day continuous stage riding. We are indeed roughing it. At 3:15 last rig crossed the Big Horn River. Our afternoon drive was a very hot one, we crossed several ranges of bluffs, with parched sands, cactus and sage brush for our only sights. At 8:40 we reached Otto, a small town on "Grey Bull," and pitched our tents for the night; most of our party

took tea up town, I shipped two horned toads to-day;
to W. A. Grove, Tipton, Iowa, and Ray Herrell, New
London, Iowa. The boys had beer and a jolly good
time. Otto is a little town; they anticipate a county
seat here this year; the people treated us royally. It
looks wild and weird here in the "Big Horn Basin." We
were glad to reach a little town, we all gave a cheer
when we beheld the city; went to bed at 10:45 P. M.

WEDNESDAY.

This morning the people of Otto came out to visit
us, they appear social and full of all kinds of energy.
In this country wherever you find water you find
people, the country is dull, no railroad and little business of any kind, the people appear to be anxious to
sell, but find little or no encouragement. You can buy
town lots for $10.00 and up; if they succeed in getting
county seat their property will advance and make a
few of them rich. We left camp at 8:30 and drove through
the desert until noon passing only two little shanty houses;
at dinner we camped on Gray Bull Creek, a poor place,
poor water, poor shade, and sun scorching hot; we
stopped three hours. At 3:15 we were off again, the
afternoon was cool when compared with forenoon, we
made good time, found some fine specimens of onyx,
shot some sage-hens, and tried to shoot some prairie
dogs. In the evening we camped at a lonely place in the
desert; the first thing we did was to kill a few large
and yellow-spotted rattle-snakes, they were fierce; we
called this camp "Camp Rattle-Snake." I found a large
and beautiful moss agate, the largest I ever saw, worth

probably $50.00 in the rough. Had rabbit and grouse as wild flesh for supper. The boys played cards and smoked, the ladies and few men told stories; went to bed at 10:10 and slept well among the rattlesnakes.

THURSDAY.

We could not wash our faces out of the filthy pools in the ravines, the water was warm, dirty and filthy. It is hard to travel over a large desert on account of scarcity of water; we are on the desert now for three days and it will take us three days more to cross; this desert is more than 100 miles wide, where I write this letter we are many, many miles from any other living people as far as we know. At 6:30 we left camp and moved boldly to the north-west, a little rain the day before and a cool breeze for a change in the morning made it more pleasant to-day. I killed a rattle-snake and took off six rattles; we saw prairie dogs and buffalo skeletons all along the way. At 12:20 we reached a little town named Corbett, on Stinking Water River; here we found a post-office, saloon, hotel and a little store all in one little building; we took dinner here and drank beer. I wrote one letter and nine postal cards. This was a fearful hot place, the people here enjoyed our visit. At 2:30 we left for an afternoon ride. It rained a little about 3:30, and we drove along steadily until 6:45 P. M., then went into camp at base of Heart Mountain. We soon had our tents pitched and were ready for supper. We are getting to base of Mountains now, it is getting cooler and water is getting better. Hail! The cool mountains and good water. We saw a place where a man had killed four antelopes and skinned them, and left the skins on the ground. Our camp to-night was located at a lovely place. We found many beautiful flowers in the woods. At places the pines are very thick, I noticed at one place that pines were lying eight on top of each other that had been blown down by the wind. After supper we looked at the moon and stars, had some music and stories, then went to bed at 10:45 and had a cool and pleasant sleep.

FRIDAY.

Breakfast on potatoes, eggs, pork, oat meal and biscuits. At 7:45 we resumed our journey and passed rapidly up the mountains. The road was very hilly and rough, we had to walk quite a distance, on some of the hills we had to double team and put on six horses; on the way we stopped at Chapman's Ranch, who controls 10,000 acres of land, 6,000 head of cows and and 1,000 head of horses, and has 10 large stacks of hay. Mrs. Stark here received a lovely bouquet of flowers.

We pulled on until 3:30 when we reached the summit of Dead Indian Hill then stopped for the night; here we met two companies going to Yellowstone National Park. The outlook from the summit is extraordinary, to the north and west the view is unlimited. We can now see the great Basin and desert we passed over. We had a pleasant afternoon. We took dinner at 5:30, then took a stroll over the hills. We had a very pleasant camp; most all camp talk now is Free Silver and Tariff. The ladies treated us to nice bouquets; we had a beautiful view of sun set, two beautiful camp fires, told stories, then went to bed at 10:45.

SATURDAY.

This morning we started on the hardest journey of the whole journey; going down several hills almost straight down for miles, every one of our party had to walk, the wagons locked all four wheels, then cut a large tree and tied it behind each wagon and then started on our perilous journey; it was fearful; I traveled over many mountains but the west side of Dead Indian Hill beat anything I ever saw. At noon we camped at Dead Indian Creek, here we rested and refreshed for the afternoon journey. We also met a second party who camped here on their way to the Yellowstone.

At 3.30, and we were moving; we passed up and down some very bad hills. At one place we had to tie ropes to our wagons and have five strong men to hold them, to keep the wagons from rolling down the mountains into the valleys. We encountered a hard shower of rain this afternoon. The scenery along the way was magnificent, in places high peaks lifted their cruel serrated summits up into the blue sky. In the distance were the eternal hills covered with perpetual snow, beautiful landscapes, rocky cliffs and fine terraces; uplands sloping decked the mountain side, and evergreen over evergreen in gay theatric pride; we passed through a beautiful natural park late in the afternoon; the valley is almost level and hemmed in by great rocky peaks. At 6:30 we landed on Beam's Horse Ranch, on Sunlight River. The cook baked biscuits and furnished us an elegant supper at 8:30. The evening was very damp, the night was cold and made us think of home.

SUNDAY.

Breakfast at 5:10. We had a heavy frost during
the night. This is Sunday morning in the mountains,
far, far away from the active world. The company
packed early for the trip, every one appears to be happy.
One can scarcely get enough of sleep and enough to eat
in the mountains. This trip is an immense tonic for
the whole party; no sick one in the whole company
thus far. This Sunday forenoon was spent in getting
back to fording place. The river was swift and strong
and hence we had to go towards head water of the
stream, then drive directly back on the other side. It
took us one day to travel ten rods on our trip. After
we left camp we got into the hills and swamps that
was indeed a sight. In places it took six horses to pull
a light load and five to six men holding on with ropes
to hold wagons from rolling down the mountains; at
one place where the rocks had rolled down from a high
peak, boulders were strewn along so thick that it
looked impossible for any team to pass over; everyone
walked and empty wagons got over safely. We saw a
beautiful cataract, where the wide Sunlight River passed
swift and strong through a narrow canyon. I went on
top in company with Mr. Record. The cold compressed
air fanned us beautifully. We passed down some nice
gulleys and halted for dinner on a nice little creek,
tributary to Sunlight and Clark Rivers. We had a good
dinner, nice sport and a little nap.

At 2:15 we started again on our journey. Great
Heavens!!! This afternoon trip beat Halifax and
Jerusalem thrown in! About 3:30 we started to go

down a west range of the Shoshone Mountains. Eight teams in our procession, and a road that is terrific. We had a sore time the past two days, but this beat them all. The road is bold, rough, rocky, steep, slanting and has sharp curves. We tied ropes to front of our wagons and one to hind part of each wagon and then put other end of rope around trees and other objects that were along side the road, and then that end was held by three to five men, and in this way we worked our eight teams down the mountain. I walked up and down the mountain about four times trying to help the teams. I was afraid we would be dashed to pieces. In places you could see pieces of wagons down along the sides of the mountains; wagons that had slipped off the roads and dashed down over the sides of the mountains.

This was a dreary Sunday afternoon. I did not work as hard for many years as I worked this afternoon. No Church or Sunday-school this day. The scenery along the mountains was sublime; in places you could see large bold knobs lift their heads high into the heavens. Everyone appeared tired when they came into camp at 7:15. We soon had our tents placed and a large mosquito fire built up. This camp the ladies named Stoneybrook on Stoneycreek, a beautiful stream of clear cold water. One of our drivers shot at a deer near our camp. We had a good supper at 8:20. The evening was spent in telling camp-fire stories; the camp is on a little plain along side of a big mountain. On the right is the valley with Clark River below, on the left are the high peaks of the Rockies,

on the rear and in front are immense tracts of thick
ever-green. You might say we camped in a little pocket
in the mountains. The night was cold and frosty.

MONDAY.

This morning we washed in an ice cold creek. We
soon had our beds packed and tents rolled up and
started. This makes our thirteenth day since we started
from Ottumwa, and my sixteenth day since I left
Tipton, Iowa. We were to go through on stage line
from Sheridan, Wyoming, to Yellowstone National Park
in six days. Thus we will be about ten or eleven days
over due going out.

Now how about time in the Park and coming back?
This is by far the grandest trip of my life; the scenes
among these lonely and non-inhabited mountains is
grand, beyond all imagination. We passed some large
herds of cattle; met some people from St. Louis, Mo.,
on their way into the mountains to find precious
metals; we saw quite a lot of dead cattle that probably
perished in the cold winters of Northern Wyoming;
saw a flock of wild ducks on one of the several
Mountain Lakes that we passed. The road in places
is intensely swampy, several springs empty their
contents onto the side plains and make the roads almost
impassable. We passed beautiful groves of "Quaking
Asp," saw many beautiful rocky castles, rounded as by
art. We forded Clark River where the water reached
the side of the wagon box. The creeks we passed over
this forenoon had fearful rocky bottoms. We camped
at noon along side of a quiet mountain where we

had good water; the company in my wagon had plenty
of beer and whiskey and of course I did not suffer any.
We broke rear spring on our wagon this forenoon, but
had it fixed at noon; the mosquitoes and flies were very
bad in the warm swampy hollows.

We have a very skillful driver on our commissary
wagon, he drives four horses and goes through places
that one can scarcely walk through; in places we make
our own roads and again we find abandoned roads,
also roads used only a few times in a year. I did not
shave now for nearly two weeks, had no opportunity;
we are getting pretty seedy, have not changed shirts
since July 2, this is July 21, the dirt is beginning to
wear off. Had no mail for same time, expect none for
three weeks to come, did not write any postal cards
for over one week, because we did not meet any one
going to some Railroad town; last week we would pass
teams occasionally going to some distant town for
provisions, by which we could send mail that would
reach some Railroad.

This forenoon we had an extremely hot sun, and
made a short camp at noon; we passed several nice
water-falls, cascades, immense areas of trees; we went
up a very bad hill, crossed a river and passed a few
beautiful lakes; the mosquitoes and horse flies were
very bad, they almost ate us up. We made a long
heavy drive, saw a mountain peak that shot its spires
high into the clouds; saw and passed snow. In the
evening at 8:01 we reached Cook City, Montana, a
small and almost deserted mining camp, nearly all of
their houses had the windows nailed shut. It is too
cold to raise anything here, you do not see a garden

any place; the people look poor. We have snow all around us this night, the air is cold and damp. Had supper at 9:20; wrote letters and postal cards; tents pitched, beds made and slept our first night in Montana.

TUESDAY.

A few of our party took their meals up town. The people here are decidedly for free silver, it is all they have. We remained in Cook City several hours for repairs. This is the first town of any size that we struck for more than a week, The people in Cook City are quite sociable. At 9:30 we started on the trip, we passed rapidly on and at 11 A. M. reached the limit of the much talked of Famous Yellowstone National Park. They had rules posted at the entrance so each one could read rules about hunting, fishing, and carrying specimens out of park. We passed magnificent scenery, great high mountains of rocks covered with everlasting snow, while here and there you could see a beautiful stream of water leaping down the mountain's side. The scenery cannot be described; one must see it to enjoy it; the roads in places in the park were bad, they had some great wash-outs. As I sit and write this, I see a mighty Peak right in front of me, named "Longfellow," and to left of me is the great Norris Peak. At noon we halted in a shady spot on Soda Butte Creek, the air was cool and all nature invigorating. We sat among the shades of the trees and ate our dinners. In the afternoon nature kept growing more sublime and the scenes more varied. Early in the evening we halted at Soda Butte; nearly all the men started for a mountain lake to catch trout; we only caught a few but they were nice, the finset I ever ate, the meat was as red as blood, and solid and sweet; all trout are so that live in cold mountain torrents. The mosquitoes were bad, they almost ate us up while at the Lake fishing. Will Thomas was quite sick in camp this evening.

WEDNESDAY.

The night was cold, ice froze in the camp July 22. The location for camp was beautiful. We watched a lovely sun-rise; we all nestled very closely to fire, cold! cold!! cold!!! We left camp at 7:40, were soon met by a private soldier who sealed all of our fire-arms so we could not shoot any of the game in the park; he tied a red ribbon around hammer and trigger, then tied a knot, melted red wax on this knot and while it was hot pressed a United States stamp upon it, so no one could use their fire-arms unless detected. The penalty for removing any relics, defacing park, and molesting any of the animals is $2,000 fine, and two years in penitentiary.

I got a fine specimen of soda-stone from an extinct Geyser, adjoining this was a fine soda spring, where I filled a beer bottle to take along to Iowa. We saw two antelopes near the road; passed several beautiful mountain lakes. The day so far is cool and the scenery magnificent; we camped at noon at *Petrified Forest* where we saw the finest rock formation; had dinner on ham, hot biscuits, tomatoes and fruit. We started again at 3:20, our first stop was at Yancy's Ranch, where we had some beer and milk. Mr. John Yancy is proprietor of Pleasant Valley Hotel. He has 10 acres leased from the government. He keeps a few cows. We here passed several parties going out into the mountains to fix roads. We also passed over Yellowstone River, swift, deep and strong, at 4 P. M. Drove up a fearful steep hill about three miles long, it was all two horses could do to pull up an empty wagon and stop about every one hundred feet.

The scenery to-day was not as nice as usual. We camped at 6:30 at "Black Deer Tail Creek." It rained a little in the evening and made it a little unpleasant for us. I found some fine petrified stone. A few of the party found some fine onyx. We can see snow on the mountains all around us. I drove most of this afternoon. We spent a horrible night in camp. Soon after we had our tents pitched and beds made it commenced to rain. Our cook had supper about ready when the rain came and washed away the fire and our supper. It rained and hailed furiously. In a short time the mountains looked as if it had snowed. The rain came through the tents and formed a little lake, the water came through the canvas and soaked our clothing and our beds. About 9:00 the rain ceased. The cook prepared supper again and just as supper was ready the second time, it commenced to rain harder than the first time. The few that ventured out got a hot biscuit and ran into the tent and ate it. The majority had no supper. I got two biscuits and a piece of meat at 10:15. The rain kept pouring down in torrents. We nestled closely together and kept singing songs, smoking, and telling stories till midnight. Our beds were wet but we crawled into them and slept a little. My back was in a little pool of water. A white coat of frost was over our bed clothes in the morning.

This is horrible on high mountains and a freezing temperature, enough to kill everyone in our camp. We had a good dose of whisky and then cut wood to get warm. It rained until 4 o'clock the next morning. During all this fearful night not one of our party complained.

THURSDAY.

Hail! See the approaching sun. Mr. J. W. Law, one of our party from Bloomfield, Iowa, made fire, and we all had breakfast at 9:30. It took us nearly all morning to get our clothes dry and feet warm. At 10:30 our camp moved. We passed through canyons, gulches, over hills, through mud holes until 2:40 P. M., when we reached Mammoth Hot Springs, Yellostone National Park, one of the principle features of our trip. We saw many animal tracks, two fine water falls and passed down a fearful hill to get to the Springs. The tents were soon pitched and we had dinner at 5:10.

The Springs here are indeed fine. There are more than 1000 active springs in the Park. The Mammoth Hot Springs alone cover 640 acres. In places the water boils out of the earth as big around as a rain barrel and very hot, probably 400° fahr. The soda formations around the springs are fine. The sulphur forms yellow; soda white; oxides, red. At one place you could see a whole ridge of boiling pots and spouting Geysers, some spurted up about 6 feet.

A great many people are here viewing the sights. The Park is under the strictest military control. We had our guns sealed three days ago. But here they took them all from us. They have a "Mammoth Hotel" here, and a Cottage Hotel; they are under the control of a Stock Company from Ohio. Their rates are $4.00 per day. You cannot buy anything here outside of hotels. In the evening we had a fine bath in a hot lake in the hills and visited an extinct Geyser called the "devil's kitchen." We went down into this on a ladder about 40 feet. It was quite hot and dark at the bottom. In the evening we visited several camps and the city proper. I purchased 100 pictures of the different things in Park. Went to camp and had lunch and beer, then went to bed at 11 P. M.

FRIDAY.

We were awakened by a sunrise salute of cannon. After breakfast we went down in front of "Mammoth Hot Springs Hotel" and there watched the U. S. officers drill their cavalry and infantry. I met Mr. Stiver, a photographer, who was raised only 14 miles from Clarence, Iowa. He sold us some fine views and gave us information about the Park. We were also introduced to two Scott brothers, who entertained us.

We did some writing, bought guide books of the Park, then packed our tents and got ready to start about noon. We had nearly a whole day at Mammoth Springs. Everywhere you look the scenery is bewildering. We took luncheon at 12:20. Then started for Norris Basin, 20 miles away. We first passed Golden Gate, costing $14,000 per mile to construct the road around a cliff. A beautiful water fall 160 feet high is at far end. We passed a number of lakes, peaks and short ranges. At "Apollinaris Springs" we had a delightful drink, also filled our bottles to take home. "Obsidian Cliff," of almost solid glass was very

picturesque with variegated streaks of red and yellow.
When they built the road they could not use powder,
so a big fire was built on the rocks of glass of volcanic
action, and rocks expanded, then cold water suddenly
dashed upon it and cracked them into pieces. The glass
is very hard. The indians used to make their arrows
out of this kind of rock. On Beaver Lake we saw a
beaver house and numerous water fowl. We passed a
hot spring called "Frying Pan," on account of its
peculiar noise, we saw at least 60 hot springs to-day.
We like our trip fine; we are now in the Norris Geyser
Regions. I can hear them roar this evening, as I write
this, it sounds like roar of a distant thrashing machine.
We camp to-night in Norris Basin, 20 miles from
Mammoth Hot Springs. The Government roads in
Park are very fine. We pitched tents at 6:30 and had
supper, About twenty-five tents filled with strangers
were here on these commons. We had a lively time
visiting camps.

SATURDAY.

We had breakfast on oatmeal and fried mush. The
earth was blanketed under a white frost this morning.
At 6:10 we passed into the Norris Geyser Basin, cover-
ing six miles square, and alive with hot Springs and
spouting Geysers. We first visited "Congress Geyser,"
40 feet in diameter. The water is pale blue and boils
furiously. The Constant Geyser discharges every
minute. The "Black Growler" throws off very little
water, but an enormous amount of steam producing a
peculiar sound. The "Emerald Pool" is 40 x 50 feet,
and boils violently. The "New Crater Geyser" came
into prominence in 1893, and sends forth a great

volume of boiling water and steam. It erupts every 30 minutes. "The Monarch Geyser is the grandest in this basin. It erupts every 12 hours. We were lucky enough to see it explode; we were about one quarter of a mile away; the waters were forced up at least 100 feet, There are at least 1000 Geysers and Hot Springs in this Basin. Elk Park, Gibbon Canyon, Gibbon Falls 80 feet high, and the Paint Pots were intensely interesting and pleasing. We passed several mineral springs, soda and sulphur; and a goodly number of tourists.

The drive this forenoon was excellent; we drove too fast and our commissary wagon could not catch up with us, so we had to buy an extra dinner at a store. We halted at 2 P. M., and started again 3:30. Our first visit was the "Fountain Geyser," which erupts at intervals of 2 to 4 hours, and throws water 60 feet high. After its action the water falls back about 18 inches; this must be filled up again before another eruption can take place. "Clepsydra Spring" displays so violently that it is called "The Spouter." The Mammoth Paint Pots, where you can see a continuous boiling of mud, producing sounds like a hoarse "plop plop," and of various colors are exceptionally fine. The "Great Fountain Geyser," the "Great Fountain," the "White Dome," "Surprise," "Fire Hole Spring," and "Mushrom," are of great interest, On "Midway Geyser Basin" we visited the "Excelsior Geyser" and "Hell's Half Acre," where the whole earth is under a tremendous fire. "Turquois Spring, a green hot spring. "Prismatic Lake," a lake that reflects the colors of the rainbow, were next visited. At 6:30 we passed into "Upper Geyser Basin" containing some 60 Geysers and

409 Hot Springs with all marvels of beauty. Clouds
of vapor over-hang this valley. The earth trembles
and is filled with strange rumblings; it looks like an
addition to "Dante's Inferno." "Old Faithful Geyser"
erupts every 63 minutes and shoots its boiling water
up 150 feet. We camped close to this one for the night.

The "Cascade Geyser" erupts every 10 minutes,
when the water is forced upwards 30 to 40 feet. The
"Bee Hive Geyser," 4 feet in diameter, erupts every 4
hours, and shoots up its water 220 feet, The "Giantess
Geyser" with an opening of 8 feet in diameter erupts
at intervals of fourteen days; the eruption lasts twelve
hours; this is the grandest Geyser in the known world;
here the water heated to 450° fahrenheit spouts up as
if by magic 250 feet. The "Sponge," "Lion," "Lioness"
and "Cubs," The "Grand and Turban" erupts at
stated intervals of 10 minutes to 4 hours and throw
their waters from 10 to 200 feet, The "Economic
Geyser" throws its waters straight up, then falls
directly back without overflow, hence the name. The
"Giant Geyser" erupts twice per week and throws its
water 200 feet up into the air. The "Otto," the
"Grotto," the "Riverside," the "Fan and Mortar," the
"Splendid," the "Punch Bowl," all excited the admira-
tion of our company on account of their peculiar color,
marvelous formation, bad odors, regular periods of
action and terrific ways of spouting.

In the evening E. O. Spielberg and I took an extra
side trip of about four miles and visited "Black Sand
Basin" and "Specimen Lake," "Sunlight Basin" and
"Cliff Geyser," "Castle Geyser" and "Bee Hive,"
"Morning Glory Spring and Geyser," "Artemsia,"

"Biscuit Basin" and "Jewel Geyser." These all are great Springs or Geysers and have their peculiarities. The "Gem Spring" is a beauty, it is large, green and has beautiful sides. If you throw anything into the Spring it becomes coated and looks very beautiful. This whole county is under fire; it sounds hollow if you strike the earth. Had supper and went to bed at 10:30.

SUNDAY.

We saw "Old Faithful," "Lion" and "Cascade" erupt almost at the same time. You can see rainbows and almost any kind of designs. We had a beautiful stroll over the various formations. It is very dangerous in places; we camped at a very picturesque place. We washed in hot spring water. You can see large crowds of people come out to see these Geysers erupt; they nearly all erupt at regular intervals so they know just when to go. The hotels at these places are fine, lighted up by electricity, and heated and operated by steam. (As I am writing this "Old Faithful" is going off about 10 rods to my right. Do you hear it?) At 9 A. M. we started on a trip through Upper Geyser Basin to Yellowstone Lake. The first place of interest was Keppler's Cascades where the Madison River leaps from shelf to shelf over a rocky chasm in a series of enchanting falls 100 to 150 feet high. The roads up through these mountains are graded as regular as a Grand Trunk Railway. In places you ascend the mountain and you do not know it. We had a beautiful view of Shoshone Lake from a commanding point high up in the mountains.

Our drive this forenoon was pleasant; we passed through some beautiful canyons. Our first view of Yellowstone Lake, as we were passing down the side of the Mountain was simply grand. We halted at noon at West Thumb Lunch Station, situated on the Lake, pitched our tents and had dinner at 4:30. I did a big lot of writing to-day. After supper we went to fish on the Lake; the trout were very plenty but would not bite; we saw where the fish were so plentiful that people killed them with clubs; we caught a few fine trout. On our way home we saw three deers; they were quite tame; they walked to the side of the road and commenced to eat grass as we passed. We saw a place where people could catch fish in Yellowstone Lake and boil them in a cone of a boiling Geyser without moving a step. The hot spring and lake have no connection whatever. We tented at a very beautiful place where we could overlook the lake in fine shape; if you stand on the shore of the lake you can see schools of trout. We chased a bear away from camp this afternoon, the bears are plentiful here and quite tame; no one is allowed to shoot or molest them in Park, besides our fire arms were all taken from us when we entered the Park proper, and thus the animals could torture us as they pleased.

In the evening our party chased several bears out of the camp. We went to bed at 9:30; about 2 o'clock at night I heard a racket in front of the the tent, when lo! two big bears had robbed our wagon, stole our meat and were in front of our tent eating it; one had crawled up a tree, I whistled for a dog then they walked away over the hill. In the morning a deer came into camp; we had a good look at it, then it ran away.

MONDAY.

We had a good breakfast on trout. I wrote a large letter for *New London Sun*. We had a pleasant drive along the lake all day, camped on its banks at noon and had another fine mess of trout. At 3:50 we reached Lake Hotel; here our party saw a steamer come in from West Thumb. They had four buffaloes at this place. We camped on the Yellowstone River. The boys caught an immense lot of trout to-night; the banks of the river were fairly lined; we had three camp-fires and plenty of stories in the evening.

TUESDAY.

We had breakfast principally on trout, some four of our boys were trout-sick this morning; our cook threw away nearly one bushel of fine trout. Had a little rain here. The mosquitoes were intensely bad. We broke camp at 8:10 and drove along the Yellowstone River, viewing the fine river, fine Hayden valley, fine evergreen forests, hot springs and a mud volcano where the mud keeps on working back into the crater until it almost chokes the working of the volcano. The smell at some of these hot springs is very disagreeable. The Cascade Falls, Upper and Lower Falls of Yellowstone and Grand Canyon, Lookout Point and Sulphur Mountain, are beyond description.

We shall never forget our first view of the Grand Canyon from Grand View; it rained pretty heavily as our party was viewing this sublime chasm but no one appeared to notice it. This Canyon is not the grandest on earth, yet there is none more beautiful in the world. There is not the breadth and dash of Niagara nor is

there the enormous leap of the Yosemite, in the mad
rush of the Yellowstone. Here is majesty of its own
kind and a beauty too that denies description. On either
side of the river are vast pinnacles of sculptured rocks.
The shelf of rock over which the river leaps is absolutely
level and about seventy feet wide. The water seems to
wait a moment on its verge, then it passes with a single
bound 360 feet into the mighty gorge below It is a
sheer, unbroken, compact, shining mass of silver foam.
The river here flows through an appalling depth and
the falls unroll their whiteness down amid the canyon's
gloom. At Point Look Out, the over hanging cliffs are
more than perpendicular. Throw a stone over it, you
must wait long before you see it strike the water in
that awful and yawning chasm. The water dashing
there as in mad agony against those rocks and cliffs,
you cannot hear. You look on stillness, solemn as midnight, profound as death. The mighty distance lays
the fingers of silence on its white and fearful lips. The
opulence of color throughout this canyon is magnificent
and fascinating; the whole gorge flames; it is as though
rainbows had fallen out of the sky and hung themselves
there like glorious banners. The clearest yellow is below,
this flushes up into orange; down at the base the
deepest mosses unroll their draperies of the most vivid
green; browns sweet and soft do their blending; white
rocks stand spectral, turrets of rocks shoot up as
crimson as though they were drenched through with
blood. It is as if the most glorious sunset had been
caught and held resplendent over that awful gorge, ten
miles long with an average depth of 1200 feet.

Our party got very much bewildered here and
lost some of their conveyances. The Bloomfield crowd

had a big time to get back again; our load stayed
right with our driver, Mr. Record, and got through all
right.   Our party felt sorry they could not live here
and keep viewing the scenes along the Grand Canyon.
We met a camp of young ladies at Grand Canyon
Junction who called for our boys to come and eat pan
cakes with them.   The Red Oak crowd did not stop to
see the Falls on account of rain.   We did not camp
for noon but drove direct to camping ground at Norris
Basin and there pitched our tents.   The afternoon
drive was unpleasant; a cold and chilly rain will spoil
almost any drive; nearly the whole afternoon we drove
through the densest forests of evergreen.   We reached
Norris Basin at 2:20, after driving about 25 miles.
At Norris we met a company from Nebraska, Judge
John S. Robinson, James Stewart, Tom Cook, Tom
Memmiger, of Madison county, and a doctor from
Lincoln.   They were a jolly crowd; we used their camp
fires to dry our clothing; they also offered to get dinner
for us.   It rained hard when we put up our tents; we
had dinner at 4:10.   After dinner some of the boys went
into Norris Geyser Basin, some visited neighboring camp
fires, and still others remained in camp.   I wrote a letter
to *Tipton Advertiser*, also one to *Martinsburg Herald*
for publication.   In the evening after luncheon the male
part of our company visited Nebraska camp-fire and we
had a jolly time; they had a big camp-fire and we
formed a circle around it, sang songs and told stories.
We sang doxology at 10:30, then went to camp and
slept.

WEDNESDAY.

Breakfast at 6:30.   We had a very hard frost.
Packed our beds and tents and were ready to move at

8 o'clock. Our camps took a straw vote on McKinley and Bryan, McKinley carried five to one. We drove rapidly on this afternoon, stopping at Apollinaris Spring for a good drink of special water. We are returning back now on the same road that we came as far as north end of Park. Our party camped at noon at Golden Gate; the stop was short. At 2:40 we passed through Golden Gate and down the Mountains at a lively rate. We reached Mammoth Hot Springs again at 3:05; here our party had a lively time for a while, first they crowded the Post Office, next Mr. Record got our firearms out of bondage, then bought Souvenirs to take home. Some bought lovely pictures of the various formations, others bought crystallized or coated formations, and still others bought books and notions. Mr. Record galloping about on a gray horse attending to the various matters; he looked like General Meade before the battle of Gettysburg. Our party cheered when he read a letter from the obliging B. & M. R. R. officials, telling us our tickets will be sent to Billings, Montana, for return passage. We are about eight days behind time and thought we could not make Sheridan in time, so through the instrumentality of Mr. Record and others, the Burlington Railroad Co. granted us permission to take train at Billings, Montana, about 165 miles north-west of Sheridan, and ride by rail to Sheridan, so we could reach that place before the expiration of our tickets. The B. & M. road treated our company white, and we all appreciated it; we were fooled in our trip out at least eight days and now having been granted such a favor in a great need, is not a small favor. At 4:20 our party bid adieu to Mammoth Hot Springs and its marvelous beauties, and

started for Montana   We passed through a very
bluffy country but on excellent roads.   At 5:15 we
reached Gardiner City, on Montana line.   Here of course
a few of our party had to have their beer.   We escaped
a fearful rainstorm by getting out of Norris Basin in
time; we could look back into the valleys and see them
filled with black clouds.   At 6:15 we reached Cinnabar,
Montana; this is a small town like Gardiner City, a few
houses and a few saloons; here our manager bought in
a fresh supply of provisions to last us to Billings,
Montana.   We had supper here in the hotel, the first
time some of us ate at a table for over three long weeks.

Our party was divided at this place.   The Bloomfield
crowd composed of J. W. Law, Mr. and Mrs. J. W.
Stark and Miss May Allender.   Will Thomas, S. G.
Hersman and J. R. Anderson of Red Oak, Iowa, took
a Northern Pacific train for the East; some were unwell
on account of wet weather and constant driving over
all kinds of roads and through all sorts of weather for
twenty-six days; others were hurried home on account
of business relations.   We stopped a while with these
people while they were getting their baggage from our
commissary and tent wagons.   Then drove one and
one-half miles to a creek and went into camp; we put
up our tents and made our beds on the rocks.   E. O.
Spielberg and myself went to the depot and saw this
contingent   take   their   departure   from   Cinnabar,
Montana, to Iowa; the parting was somewhat sad;
we had never seen them before, have been with them
for twenty-six long days, and now we leave them and
probably never to see them again.   Our tent to-night
was in a lonely place, hemmed in by high mountains
and densely surrounded by sage-brush.

THURSDAY.

We had a fine breakfast on beefsteak and fried mush. Our horses are lost again this morning, so we got a late start. We visited a small town by the name of Hoar; this was the first business town we visited for a long while; they have several large coal mines in the hills surrounding this little town of probably 100 people. They have here 103 coke ovens in full blast; the coal is floomed down the mountain, that is, it is put into a trough and the water washes it down to the coke ovens. The coal which they ship is brought down the mountains in small cars, working on an inclined plane, so that when one car runs down loaded it draws up another empty; a brake is used to keep it from running too fast. *Cinnabar Mountain*, the Devil's Slide, almost two thousand feet straight down, and Electric Peak form natural scenic wonders that surround this lonely little hamlet.

This day we saw mountain scenery that even surpasses the mountain scenery in the Park. The strata, various in form and kind, are folded and turned into every imaginable way. We were glad we did not meet any teams, it would have been impossible to pass anyone nearly the whole way. At noon we camped at Poole's Ranch on a little creek; we wanted to get a lunch at this place, but his prices were wild, so he kept his grub and we kept our money. We made a short halt at noon, as we had no grass for our horses at this place. We camped at 1:05 and started at 2:10, and had a lovely drive in the afternoon through Paradise Valley. Saw some beautiful ranches. Had a little rain which made driving very pleasant. We passed a freight

train on the N. P. this afternoon, July 31, the first one
we saw since leaving Sheridan, Wyoming, July 9. We
passed through "Yankee Jim's Canyon" and saw
"Emigrant Peak."

Our party was divided again for staging on account
of Bloomfield and some of Red Oak party leaving us.
Jno. Finley and wife, E. O. Spielberg and myself took
the ladies' hack; Mr. Ostergard and wife took fast mail,
No. 1, with J, F. Record for engineer; wagon No. 2,
hauls Hysham and Iddings with Marion Cover holding
the lines. We passed several heavy towns this day.
Sphinx city had simply a little station and at Dailey
city only a board stuck into the ground with name on it.
The mosquitoes were fearfully bad. We are now 27 miles
from Cinnabar, at the foot of Emigrant Peak. Some
of the boys are catching trout for supper. We visited
a little grave-yard in the evening, thirteen graves
numbered them all. We had a lovely place for camp,
nice level ground and an imposing surrounding. Had
some fresh fish for supper; went to bed at 9:20, and
had a fine sleep.

FRIDAY.

Had an early breakfast. Broke camp and started
on our journey North at 7 P. M. The drive early this
morning was delightful; we are now getting out into
the world a little more. We passed through a little
town called Emigrant; a tramp jumped into our wagon
and wanted to ride along to Livingston, Montana, at
least one good day's drive, and meals furnished; we
put him off and sent him to manager, who told tramp
that manager was ahead, this settled him. Quite a
number of nice ranches dot this valley. Oats, wheat,

and Alfalfa clover are their farm productions: Their
houses are small; the people are evidently poor. The
hills and uplands, the rocks and stratas of earth made
the trip interesting and pleasant. At noon we halted
seven miles south of Livingston in a little timber. This
was a hot day, quite a change since coming down off
the Rockies where we had snow and frost on the earth.
The mosquitoes are quite bad in these Montana valleys.
At 2:05 and on we went passing several lime-kilns.
An extra engine came very near runing into our second
wagon. We passed through brushy roads and crossed
a crossing at a sharp curve just as an engine came around
the curve; I saw the engine first and gave the alarm;
they got off the track in safety. Had the engine been
running fast, the wagon would have been smashed
and its occupants killed. We saw some fine irrigating
ditches and some lonely peaks in the Gallatian Range.
The stratification and the eternal upheavels throughout
this valley are magnificent. At 3 o'clock in the
afternoon we reached Livingston, Montana, one of her
larger cities of probably 3000 people. Their business
houses are well built, modern in architecture and extra
stocked for a far away town with few people to trade.
We saw a few stores that will compare favorably with
our stores in larger cities. Each one in our party
hustled off to some place in the city and began to buy
such things as they needed. This is the largest town
our party saw for nearly one month. It was pretty
hard on beer for a while. Our manager here bought
another extra supply of provisions. The people appeared
very clever, they crowded around us and had many
questions to ask. It was quite a curiosity to them to

see a company of twenty go by stage as far as we did.
We are dirty and greasy and getting tired of our long,
long trip. We bid adieu to this lively little town at
4:30, and moved directly east along the Northern
Pacific Railroad. We passed their county Poor House,
a pride to this county. The prairie on the east is poor,
the grass is short, and wood entirely wanting. Occasionally we would find a small ranch and a little stock.

We passed another town this afternoon with not a
house in it. At 7:45 we struck camp about eight miles
east of Livingston on N. P. R. R. We had fried potatoes, bean soup, sweet cakes, meat, rice and apricots.
The mosquitoes reigned here supreme; we kept our faces
heavily veiled, and then they came very near eating us up.
We met a company of movers here from Washington,
who were on their way to eastern Missouri. Several
trains on the N. P. trans-continental R. R. passed us during
the night. It rained and stormed a little during this night.
The rocks were so plentiful here that we could scarcely
stake down our tents. It is very hard to find water and
wood over these dry plains. I had a bad pain in my
back this morning, the result of sleeping on a hard bed.

SATURDAY.

Our cook tried to frighten us this morning by call-
ing breakfast at 5:20. We left camp at 7:30. The
drive was principally through a valley along the
Yellowstone river and N. P. R. R. A large trans-
continental train passed us with eleven coaches
enroute to St. Paul, Minn. This forenoon while
passing through some narrow defiles a tug caught on
the edge of a rock and the harness tore right on

a Rocky Ledge, with Railroad almost straight down along the side. The valleys here are poor; we saw only one house all forenoon. Last night we camped on Mission Creek; this noon we camped about ten miles from Springdale, Montana, on an irrigating ditch. The weather was fearful hot, at one place it was 93° fahr. early in the day. A log school house was near by our noon camp which some of the boys visited and filled the black-board with writing; the school was not in session this being Saturday. At end of August this school closes; they have about eight months school in a year and change teachers every term; we found this information in the teacher's register.

Our afternoon drive was through a very stony valley; stones so thick that you could not set down your foot unless you would strike twelve stones. In places we could look down the valley for miles with nothing in sight save a wagon coming or going. Occasionally we would pass a dead cow; a certain kind of grass kills them if they accidentally eat it. We drove along Northern Pacific R. R. all day and saw only three trains; this shows that they do a light business.

We still catch glimpses of the Rockies as we are passing along the south side of the Cracy Mountains. At 5:45 we reached a little town on Yellowstone river named Big Timber, with a population of about 600 people. The people all came out and looked at our crowd; we halted on Main street, had beer and each one got a good supper at the Hotel. We camped in the evening on Boulder Creek, about one-half mile east of the town. We hired a special pasture and tenting ground and went into camp at 7:30; we pitched our tents, then went back again to town to take in a "Free Silver Speech" by a U. S. Senator of Bozeman, Montana. In my estimation he could not speak, and had very little enthusiasm among his audience; several tried to speak during the evening; The speaker stood on a street corner and the people stood around him on the street. Politics here are about equal. One thing I notice especially in traveling through these western towns, that in towns where they mine and have plenty of silver ore they all want Free Silver; in communities where they raise a great many sheep, like around Big Timber, they are all for McKinley and protection. One man has 57,000 sheep at this place on one ranch. We had a lively time going home from this speech; Ostergard and myself were for gold, while Spielberg, Record and Iddings were silver; we had a lively time. One can scarcely see how these people maintain their town. You may walk to edge of town and look out and see nothing but a baren earth; this is a typical western town. Went to bed at 10:30 and slept well.

SUNDAY.

We all washed in the Boulder River, then had breakfast on ham, fried potatoes, doughnuts, oatmeal, tea and coffee; we had the best breakfast, best camp and best surroundings of any place since we are on our great trip. We camped on a green nook and on the banks of the lovely Boulder. The sky this morning is clear and the atmosphere is invigorating. This is Sunday morning, far, far away from our accustomed places of worship; this makes our fourth Sunday among the mountains. We drove again through a very monotonous country this forenoon. We are beginning to get away again from the mountains now and into the head of "Big Horn Basin," with no grass, parched grounds and scarcely any habitation. Mr. Spielberg and I had the whole Hack to ourselves so we slept nearly all Sunday forenoon. We saw people work to-day just as on a week day in Iowa. It is quite lonely for us to ride over these desolate plains on a very hot and quiet day; you cannot imagine it, you must experience it. We camped at noon on Sweet Grass Creek, in Sweet Grass County, twelve miles east of Big Timber, on Bartell's Ranch. We met a company at this place from British America on their way to Rawlins, Wyoming. During the afternoon we passed through a Canyon where a man was buried who had six bullets in his body; he got into trouble with another man with the above results. Quite a number of abandoned shanties were noticed all along the way; men had started here, spent all their money, then had to leave.

We pressed steadily on until 7 P. M. when we found a little water on Andrew's Ranch, where we pitched our tents. The boys killed a large rattlesnake with eleven rattles, as an introduction to camp. The rattlesnakes here are yellow, and look much like the buffalo grass and cactus. One must be very careful as this snakeship has a deadly bite. At night a ranchman came into our camp and tried to sell us a lot of cattle; you can buy cattle here at almost any price. A herdsman rode up a mountain with us, who had a fine dog along that did most of the work; he was trained almost like a man. We are camping to-night in a very, very lonely place; we can look out over the sage brush and see

that we are completely hemmed in by mountains; quite
a change now when compared to rocks, frost and
mountains of last week. But oh! the loneliness of these
dreary places; had it not been for Ostergard and his
gold talk, Iddings and his free silver, Spielberg and his
religion, and Record and the ladies, some of us probably
would have perished in those arid regions.

MONDAY.

Here we had a lovely sunset and a magnificent
sunrise. We broke camp at 7:10 and drove down to the
Yellowstone River and followed the river nearly all
forenoon. At 11:10 we reached Columbus, Montana;
here our party made a rush for the stores to buy gum,
crackers, cheese, tobacco, candy and stationery.
Columbus is a lovely little town, situated among the
bleak and barren hills along the Yellowstone. The
town numbers about 250 people; how they exist is a
mystery to us. It is quite bluffy along the river, and in
places the dust is quite thick. We camped three miles
east of Columbus on a little bottom along the Yellowstone. Just as we were going into Columbus we saw
a nice flock of sage hens in the road; our party had
only a few cartridges left, which they soon used up, then
we made use of stones. I had my revolver sealed as
yet but soon broke the seal and was ready for business
when they were all gone. We drove about 21 miles
this forenoon; the brakes on our wagon were no good
so we went down the hills on a gallop. We passed
worm-fences to-day that were built up of big logs
probably 50 feet long, and 8 to 12 inches in diameter.
This valley is pretty well irrigated. So ne fair ranches too

are found here; but the mosquitoes here are fearful!!
terrific!!! The ranchmen build up fires in the cattle
yards so they can milk their cows. We passed a little
town called Merrill, that had only a little ticket office,
the only building in town. Late in the evening we
drove through an almost deserted town named Park
City; this town had probably 60 houses and only 35
people; the depreciation of tariff on wool drove them
away. We caught a few glimpses of Big Horn Mountains again this day. We had great sport shooting rabbits
this forenoon; I shot six times at one and the rabbit
ran away. Quite a heavy rain passed around us to
the north. We pitched camp about one mile east of
Park City on an irrigating ditch. We drove 36 miles
to-day, and passed some irrigating ditches that cost
many hundred thousand dollars; they were as large as
small rivers and saved a whole valley to agriculture;
they lead the water across ravines in large flumes that
are about 20 feet wide by 4 feet deep and nearly full
of water; it makes an enormous trough. I must quit
writing now, as the mosquitoes are almost eating us
alive. We had supper on fresh fish, rabbits and new
potatoes. The night was stormy and gloomy, and
mosquitoes galore.

TUESDAY.

Breakfast was called at 6:10; we ate oatmeal, hot
biscuits, tomatoes, pork, tea and coffee. It looked very
much for rain this morning, but it came not. This was
probably our last night in camp. Our camp was out
on the prairie where the wind had full sway. We
packed or beds for the train and may ride in passenger
coaches hereafter. A young man, an entire stranger,
brought us a nice chunk of ice last night.

At 8 o'clock we broke camp and moved toward the
east. Our drive this forenoon was horrible; in the early
part of the day the mosquitoes were so thick that they
fairly lined our carriages; we all rode with our faces
and hands heavily veiled and then kept up a vigorous
fight with them with brushes held in our hands; we
have often heard of mosquitoes but never saw any
before; we have heard of them being pestilent but were
never annoyed before. It seems those valleys along
their little warm streams are blocked full with these
precious little creatures. When they beheld our wagons
they closed right in on us and made a desperate fight
for our blood. About 9:30 a stiff breeze sprang up and
drove away the little creatures, that gave us so much
music and so much fight, and filled the valleys with
dust and made it far worse for us than in the morning.
We never saw any dust before; it was simply fearful!
the more fearful!! the most fearful!!! of anything we
ever saw. It seemed that Mudjekeewis broke loose from
his seat of mischief and disturbance and swallowed up
in mad fury the Wabun, the Shawondasee and the
Kabibonokka and came down the valley after us in
his frenzy, whirling and drifting the sands together as a
great "Storm Fool," wrapping us up as in a cloud.
We wore colored goggles and veils and then in places
we could not open our eyes; we experienced much hard-
ship in breathing for a distance of eleven miles. But
we grew not weary in our doings and strove on
manfully through such conditions until we reached
Billings, Montana, at 11:40 A. M. Oh! how glad we
were to reach this city of about 3,000 people. Here we
are going to quit staging; we are booked for six days

more but are worn out by dust, mosquitoes and much riding. The balance of our party takes train here for the east, Aug. 6, at 11:30 A. M. We put up at Cottage Inn Hotel; after dinner we got a general cleaning up. No one ever saw a crowd that looked worse than we did; we have been on wagons now for nearly five weeks and are glad to reach the terminus of the B. & M. R. R.

At 4:20 we bid good-bye to our livery people and cooks who were so kindly caring for us during this great trip; it was sad to give them good-bye. No one of us will probably ever see them again; they treated us as best they could; the whole company seemed pleased with the treatment we received from those Sheridan fellows. I wrote several letters here as did some others of the party. We rested most of the afternoon; in the evening we took in the city nice and fair.

WEDNESDAY.

Cottage Inn, Billings, Montana, and breakfast called at 6 o'clock, and party all responded and well. We had a delightful time at this hotel. This morning we miss our tents and scarcely know how to act when we face a fine bed. For a long time we slept on the ground and cot, but thank our stars we are done; we do not know how hard we had it until we stop and think. In the morning Ostergard, Iddings, Record and myself made a call at the B. & M. ticket office where I got an extension of ten days on my ticket and two stop over privileges, one at Sheridan, Wyoming, where the whole party stopped, and another stop at Lincoln, Nebraska. The B. & M. R. R. is without a doubt the most accommodating road I ever patronized. They granted us all the privileges we demanded. We next visited their wool warehouse; the B. & M. R. R. has a large house here and they have it pretty well filled. The sheep rangers raise an enormous amount of wool along these river bottoms. Our next visit was Billings Fire Company, where everything works by electricity, the water power being located on Yellowstone River. Their large town bell is rung also by an electric armature, which we examined; then we went to the depot and investigated and checked our baggage for the east. Billings is filled with good business houses, their saloons are very plenty; you find twice as many saloons per population in the far west as you do in the east. The farming around these towns is very poor indeed, nothing but sand.

As I sit in the hotel and write this I can see the myriads of bluffs that surround this town. At 11:30 our party partook of luncheon then went to depot. At 12:20 we bid good-bye to Billings, Montana, and started south-east. The day was fair and the sun was very hot; we made an excellent run, and passed Custer's Battle Field about 3:30, where we saw a monument on top of the hill where Custer fell; and surrounding this monument were grave-stones marking exactly the place where each soldier fell. Custer had been following a lot Indians, he thought probably twelve hundred according to trail; on a little hill where monument now stands, he sent a company of soldiers under Capt. Reno around the hill one way, while Custer himself with about 260 soldiers went around the hill another way, thinking he could attack the Sioux Indians and be reinforced by Reno for any emergancy; but his scheme sadly failed;

just as he moved around the hill the Indians met him, not 1200 as he thought, but almost 6000 Sioux warriors, who surrounded Custer completely, and cut him and his little band all to pieces; not one soul was left to tell the exciting tale. The Indian Chief cut the heart out of Custer's brother and ate it raw. The battle lasted long enough for a hungry Indian to eat his dinner, or a tallow candle to burn down one-half inch, so the Indians say. One soldier tried to escape and he was cut down, and now only a lonely marble slab marks the spot on the distant hill. Capt. Reno and his men did not reach Custer at all; had they reached him in time they might have staid the tide of the battle. Strange thoughts pass over the tourist as he gazes upon the battle-field of those heroic dead. The Crow Indian Reservation was intensely interesting; for 105 miles we passed through their reservations; they were plowing, cutting grain, making hay, herding cattle, and doing a general farm work. You could see old squaws out in the field alone loading hay into a sort of a box ladder. I saw one squaw run a self-binder. Their reservation looks fine; white "tepies" line the reservation for many miles. The Crow Indians have many horses, sheep and cows. At Crow Agency City the U. S. Government has a number of soldiers to keep the Indians from committing depredations. We passed through Parkman, a little town, that we saw burn up when we were crossing the Big Horn Mountains on our way out nearly five weeks before.

At Ranchester a gentleman named Dodge, brought us our mail. I had nearly a bushel; several more of our party got their mail the same way. The country from

Billings to Sheridan, 165 miles, is poor; the government feeds the indians and educates them, and the little farming they do does not amount to much.

At 3:42 we reached Sheridan, Wyoming; from this place we started on our big Park Expedition, July 7. It is now August 9; what a time and what a trip, and what an area we surrounded in this trip of all trips. We were all glad to get back again to Sheridan. Thos. Ostergard and wife, E. O. Spielberg, J. F. Record and myself stayed over one day; the rest pulled for their homes in Iowa as fast as they could. Sheridan is quite a new town, it had some lively booms but now it is apparently dead. Our party had a good time here with these good people. Real estate is worth only about one-fourth of what it used to be. I met Mr. Dodge, the partner of our driver at his livery barn; we had a pleasant visit with him and his friends.

THURSDAY.

Most of the party stayed at the Sheridan Inn. We spent our forenoon in visiting the town and looking over their farming country; they farm only by irrigation, and are too far from any market to sell at a gain. A few of the first settlers made considerable money in handling real estate, others apparently are succeeding well in other lines of business; their buildings are well built and nearly all out of stone. We shall never forget Sheridan and our stay at the Sheridan Inn.

At 3:15 we left the depot with Engine No. 102 and Train No. 42, hauling one Pullman, one chair, one combination and one baggage car; with engineer Tom Haley, fireman Shanon and conductor Hammon. We sped swiftly on through Wyoming, on a south-east road amidst gulches, barren hills and cattle ranches. About 5 o'clock in the afternoon all on a sudden crash our entire train came to a halt with a terrific force; we had just left Clearmont, Wyoming, and were running up a light grade at the rate of fifty miles an hour. At the head of a small curve and cut is a gulch out of which darted two steers onto the track in front of the engine; one steer kept along side of railing and was knocked back into the gulch dead; the other steer jumped in between the railings and was instantly caught by pilot and dragged along about 100 yards, when he slipped under the pilot and the "grist mill" properly commenced. The engine soon jumped the track, turned over and slid on its side along the embankment probably fifty yards further; here is where engineer escaped by throwing himself out of the window; the fireman stuck to his post a little while longer when he noticed the baggage car being forced by on his left side and water tender turn a fair summersault, when he leaped through the cab, which had top completely smashed off. The chair car and Pullman car were completely derailed and run along on the ties probably 50 yards. The commotion in the cars, the screams and shrieks of the passengers and the roar of the crash was terrific, but only lasted about 30 seconds. Not one was hurt save the engineer who was badly bruised about his shoulders, and the fireman had his right foot badly scalded. The baggage man stayed right at his post with car almost upside down and baggage all piled up on one side. It was a miracle that no one was hurt. A few were thrown out of their seats but not hurt;

myself was tossed up against a seat in front which I
grabbed firmly and shut my eyes. No one knew when
crash first came but that we might all be ground into
pieces and the cars crushed fine. When the train stopped
all made a wild rush for the outside where we beheld
a fearful sight.

The engine away off the track on its side and
sticking partly in the ground, smashed, broken
and twisted all out of shape, with a perfect cloud of
steam escaping; everything on the engine was either
broken off or twisted all out of shape. On the left side
of the engine lay the tender which had turned rear end
forward and lay on its edge with one corner sticking
down between two ties and all the trucks of first baggage car piled right on top. To the left of tender and
probably 30 feet ahead of engine and tender lay the
baggage car, making nearly a 45° angle with the track.
This car telescoped the tender completely and in doing
so was stripped of all the trucks and fixtures under-
neath. The front of baggage car struck out over the
embankment of a ravine and several feet from the
ground. The rear end was held down by the second
car which remained uncoupled, and a fearful lot of iron,
steel and wood of the wreck piled right on top. This
car was lying on one edge in a furrow which it had
plowed along side the embankment; the car was broken
and warped in bad shape. The second car had just
started to telescope when the whole train came to a
solid halt. The ties for 100 yards were cut in twain
and the rails twisted like so many willow twigs.

The appearance of the wreck is wonderful; I write
this sitting amidst the bebris. When the engine ditched,
the momentum of the train carried the tender and first

car almost on top of the engine; it looks sad to see a beautiful train smashed up into kindling wood, and also involving a fearful loss. The conductor went on ahead to next station to telegraph for another train to take us on; also telegraphed west for a wreck-train; everyone of the passengers after the wrek set to work to administer to the wounded, to put out the fires in the wreck, and do generally what they could. I got one horn and J. F. Record of Red Oak, Iowa, got the other horn of the steer that wrecked this train. I am sitting aside the wrecked engine writing this and Thos. Ostergard is sitting back of me trying to sketch the wreck. The passengers felt as if providence had surely favored them. One-half of a train smashed up with no serious injuries. It is now dusk in the wild and barren hills of Wyoming with nothing in sight, save a complete wreck and sage brush. The section men came to our aid at 6:30.

At 9 o'clock a crew came from the east and commenced to clear up in front; 10 o'clock brought the wrecking crew from Sheridan, Wyoming. They immediately set to work to put on track the coaches. They worked steadily all night. I watched them until 1:15 at night when I took a chair car and tried to sleep. At 5:10 the next morning they had worked a way through and left us out after twelve hours of delay; they put our baggage in a box car and sent us on. We got breakfast at Gillette, Wyoming. We felt a little nervous this morning; an experience like we had last evening, we do not want too often. The wreck occurred on Marshall Field's ranch, the great Chicago merchant. He has a ranch here twenty-five miles square and stocked with 30,000 head of cattle.

FRIDAY.

The display of Northern Lights or Auroraborealis was the grandest we ever saw; all kinds of figures were depicted on the northern heavens, long streamers of white shot across the sky in all imaginable ways while these again had cross streamers moving north. In the extreme north a mighty sheet shot up and remained fixed at least thirty minutes; it reminded me of a large Geyser in action along the Yellowstone.

At 5:30 in the morning, and off we were at a high rate of speed to gain lost time; we do not like this; too many cattle and gulches to do great racing. Wyoming, like Montana is indeed a dreary State; occasionally you find a little green and cattle, but the main is a dreary waste. I write this on the train, and as I look through the car window I see no living thing. At Edgemont, South Dakota, we were met again by a few of her hustling people, chief of whom I mention, H. Goddard, editor of *Express*, and Sharrock, the mayor of the city. We all made another hustle for specimens of grindstones and rosequartz. Soon we sped on again through Dakota and into north-western Nebraska. Here we met the Sand Hills and a very poor country. We had dinner at Alliance and supper at Ravenna. The ride in the afternoon was fearful fast and terrible dirty; the train was trying to gain lost time and fairly whistled across the Western Prairies; at times you could not see through the car on account of dirt and dust. Our party washed their faces at least half a dozen times to-day; we all looked like miniature darkies.

Oh! but it does one good after riding like our party over the barren and solitudes of America, to come again into a land of plenty and good civilization; one cannot help but notice the gradation in civilization as you spin east from the Buffalo Plains; first you see nothing but the domain of the prairie dogs and jack rabbit; then occasionally comes the sod house; now a little town; crops are beginning to be better, better farms and better towns, and lastly the thrifty and healthy agricultural regions of America. Eastern Nebraska is in places a veritable paradise; the finest farms loaded down with the best of natures productions. We made quite a stop at Seward, Nebraska, on account of a hot box on chair car.

SATURDAY.

We reached the depot at Lincoln, Nebraska, shortly after midnight. Ostergard and wife, Spielberg and Record went to Capitol Hotel, I went to a hotel near depot; this was our final separation. These five of our party took good-bye of one another and radiated to their respective homes. The parting was somewhat sad; we had been together quite a long time enjoying the sights and hardships in common, and now we all bid good-bye, perhaps never to see each other again. We indeed had a lovely crowd; a crowd of twenty people, under all the various vicissitudes of life that were ours, with no trouble in camp at any time, must surely be ladies and gentlemen of the highest type. Ostergard and wife, and Spielberg leave at 1:15 for their home at Newman Grove. J. F. Record stays in Lincoln one day, then goes to Glenwood, Iowa, his home; I go to Exeter, Nebraska, to visit a cousin for one week, then I go home, the last one, to Tipton, Iowa. This trip is an epoch in our lives and marks a new era.

GENERAL.

We had fifteen head of horses in our company. At the close of a day's drive they were unharnessed and turned out, the most trustworthy wearing a large bell so they could be more readily located in the morning. Only twice during our entire trip that our drivers had trouble with their horses. At West Thumb, on Yellowstone Lake, the bears and other wild animals in prowling around through the thickets that surrounded our camp, caused a stampede of our horses. About 10 o'clock at night away went our bell horse and all helter skelter down over the rocks and out through the brush. We pitied the horses yet we had to laugh. Our drivers finally succeeded in locating them about 9 o'clock the next morning. At Cinnabar, Montana, they wandered away about six miles in search of something green. It was impossible to get grass in places so the horses were kept with the wagons. Oats at feeding time was put in a nose-bag and tied to the head, then the horse would walk away a short distance and stand still and eat.

Our drivers were very kind and showed much mercy to their animals. We had one horse however that could not be trusted. E. O. Spielberg can testify to this as the pony taught him one afternoon how to turn a fair summersault and land square on the earth, with face downward. Spielberg was minus his breath and the pony minus a saddle for a short time. This was the only time during the entire trip that Spielberg looked pale. He soon managed to get the dirt out of his eyes and sand out of his mouth and moved on. In the evening the pony beat him completely; when it grew cool, he tried to put on his coat, but the pony meant "no" and gave him such an up-to-date and fantastic performance that he was glad to drop his coat and ride on and endure the elements. Rev. and Mrs. Stark, Mrs. Ostergard and Mr. Spielberg were quite fond of riding on our way out, but on returning it was seldom that any one rode. We were getting too tired, the roads too dusty and the sun too hot.

J. F. Record and J. W. Finley, were the only ones of the tourists who held on to the lines most of the way; we were short two drivers and these gentlemen offered their services free; they did well for Iowa farmers; in places all they could do was to shut their eyes and leave the wagons go on.

Our great Kodak boy was "Jimmy" Anderson of Red Oak, Iowa, who was on the alert for all the curiosities along the way. He caught a few of our party cooling their beer in the snow banks at an auspicious moment. "Jimmy" expects to hand this special picture to their minister when he gets home; he thinks that now they cannot deny their guilt. At Dead Indian Hill he had Will Thomas, S. G. Hersman, Ostergard and Spielberg climb up a very steep mountain peak and took their picture as it were above the clouds; had they slipped off the rocks in making their perilous ascent they would have furnished an interesting picture for the tent people below.

In camp we had a lovely and orderly crowd; no swearing and no carousing; a few played games, but most spent their camp time in playing tricks, telling stories and singing songs. We had an excellent cook, never saw him out of sorts once. In great rains and

storms he would stand up to his camp-fire, work and
look solemn, probably engaged in prayer that those
unwelcome clouds be rolled away, Frequently we would
sit around his fire in form of a large circle and watch
him prepare our various dishes to eat. His call to
meals was, "Come Gettee," when each one would quietly
fill his tin plate of things desired that were cooked and
walk back and sit upon the sand, grass or rock, or
whatever was convenient, and partake of a hearty
meal. The boys would not crowd, but each one was
strictly for himself. The flying sand and other dirt in
places made our light complected eatables look like if
they had been extra peppered. No one complained at
any time but that we were receiving our just share of
mineral matter. The mosquitoes in places made us
keep our faces veiled hence we experienced much incon-
venience in feeding ourselves. If we would occasionally
get hungry before meals or our indigestion poor, we
would call on Dr. Ostergard who was always extra
supplied with tonic, pabst and eatables and freely dis-
pensed with them to meet our demands. Mr. Hersman
was our hunter and kept us supplied with ground-hog,
sage-hens and rabbits; the antelope and deer could not
wait on him; while Marion Cover kept our commissary
supplied with the best mountain trout.

     In the evening each one made up his own bed as
best he could on the rock, sand, brush or whatever
the conditions of ground in camp. The ladies slept on
cots and had it much harder then we had. We prepared for bed by simply removing our coat and shoes.
Mr. Iddings would not even do this; he slept every
night with his boots on, his partner, Mr. Hysham

would occasionally scold him but it had no visible
effects. We got along very quietly in tent, especially
when we were all asleep; the only trouble then was in
snoring; we had two men along who could snore loud
enough to be heard a half mile away. Several nights
some of us laid awake half of the night under those
undesirable vibrations. No bears would then attack
us, the only danger was in rocks working loose up
among the cliffs and roll down upon the sonorous box
and close the program.

Whenever we would camp on sufficient and convenient
streams of water, you could see quite a number going
with their laundry and do their own washing; this was
especially fine while tenting among the hot springs;
the ladies in places tried to do some ironing but this
proved unsuccessful and was abandoned.

Our greatest blessing on this trip was our excellent
health. Never did any party of such number and such
a distance and over such roads and such elements pre-
vailing, come through in a better physical condition
than did this party of ours. Mr. Thomas, Mr. Law,
M. Hysham and myself had a severe cold for a few
days, this was the only physical indisposition in the
entire camp. Had we serious illness or even death, we
should not have known what to do; as in places we
were at least from six to eight days drive from the
nearest town and physician, and in places so lonely
that even the birds of the air would not visit those
devious solitudes through which we strayed—a healthy,
a happy and a blessed people.